Pueblo

Written by
R. Kent Rasmussen

Illustrated by
Kimberly L. Dawson Kurnizki

The Rourke Book Company, Inc.
Vero Beach, Florida 32964

For Bailey Kathleen Moreno, an avid reader

Printed in the United States of America

Library of Congress Cataloging-in-Publication Data

Rasmussen, R. Kent.
    Pueblo / R. Kent Rasmussen.
       p. cm. — (Native American homes)
    Includes bibliographical references and index.
    Summary: Describes the dwellings of the Pueblo Indians of the Southwest, including the rectangular buildings of stone and clay called pueblos, underground community rooms known as kivas, and cliff dwellings. Includes directions for making a model pueblo.
    ISBN 1-55916-249-X
    1. Pueblos—Juvenile literature. 2. Pueblo Indians—Juvenile literature. [1. Pueblos. 2. Pueblo Indians—Dwellings. 3. Indians of North America—Southwest, New—Dwellings.] I. Title. II. Series.

E99.P9 R17 2000
978.9004'974—dc21

00-027077

Contents

The Southwest

The only place in the United States where four different states touch each other is in the Southwest. Utah, Colorado, New Mexico, and Arizona meet at a spot called "Four Corners." It is easy to find on a map, and it is just north of where most of the Pueblo people live.

The Southwest is a high desert country. Its land is dry and rugged and has many rocky mesas. Mesas are rock hills with flat tops and very steep sides. Summer temperatures often rise above 100 degrees Fahrenheit (38 degrees Celsius). Summer nights cool down greatly. Freezing temperatures are common in winter.

A thousand years ago, there was enough rain in the Southwest for many people to live and grow crops. Later centuries had less rain, so the land could not support as many people as before. Not enough grasses grew to feed grazing animals such as buffalo. With few animals to hunt, the people living in the Southwest grew most of the food they ate.

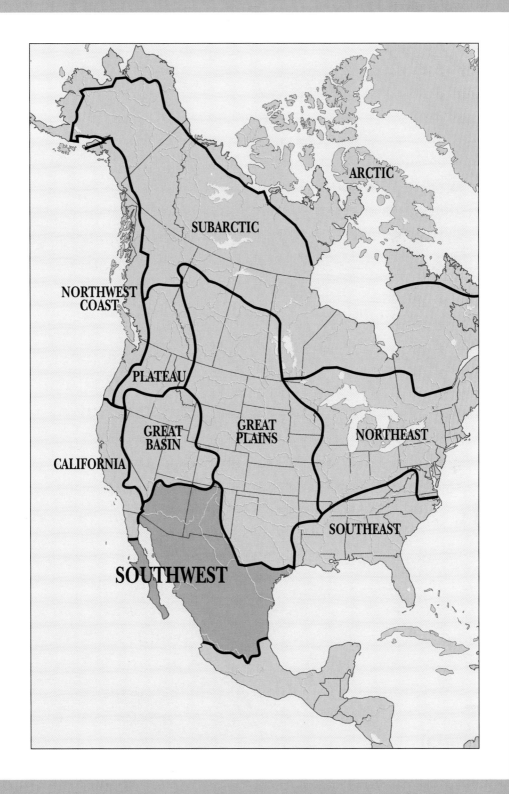

The Pueblo People

Spanish explorers first reached the Southwest during the seventeenth century. They were surprised to find local Indians living in solid, rectangular houses made of stones and *adobe,* a heavy clay. The Indians' neat villages reminded the Spaniards of their own villages, in Spain, which are called *pueblos* in Spanish.

The Spaniards felt at home in the Southwestern villages and called the Indians who lived in them *Pueblos.* Since the Indian villages are also called "pueblos," the word has a double meaning.

The Pueblo peoples are still known by their Spanish name. However, they have never been a single people. All Pueblos live in similar houses, make similar pots and baskets, and farm in similar ways. However, they actually belong to about twenty-five separate groups, or tribes. These include the Acoma, Hopi, Taos, and Zuñi. Each group is separate, and they speak different languages.

Some Pueblos are probably descendants of the mysterious *Anasazi* people, who built fine stone houses in the Southwest more than a thousand years ago.

Pueblo Buildings

Many pueblos look like modern apartment buildings.

Many pueblo buildings look like today's apartment buildings. However, they were built very differently. The many rooms of pueblos were built one at a time. Usually each room was the home of one family.

Building a pueblo always started with building one boxy room, about 12 feet wide by 20 feet long (3.5 by 6 meters). To make the pueblo bigger, builders simply attached extra rooms to the first one. Often they stacked rooms on top of one another.

Walls were made out of stone or adobe bricks. The stones or bricks were stuck together with a *mortar* made of adobe mud. Floors were usually hard clay, but sometimes they were covered with stone slabs.

The walls were thick to keep out summer heat and keep the insides cool. Rooms on the ground level almost never had outside doors. Often they had no windows, either. The early Pueblo people did not have glass and could not make windows that shut tightly to keep hot air out. When they made windows, these were only small openings, high on the walls.

Making doors that could shut tightly was also a problem. Pueblo builders did not have metal tools for woodworking until after the Spanish arrived. Instead of making doors, they left holes in the roofs. The people used ladders to climb onto their roofs and into their houses. They covered the holes with flat stones when they were not being used. They could protect their houses from enemies by pulling their ladders inside to make it hard for outsiders to get in.

Big wood beams running between the walls held up the roofs. Smaller pieces of wood were put across the beams. Above them were layers of smaller branches. Finally, thick layers of adobe mud were packed on top.

Some pueblos were as much as five stories high. Their upper rooms were usually set back from the front by the depth of one lower room. Stacked buildings looked something like huge stairs. Upper stories usually had low doorways so that people could enter from the roofs of lower floors. Outside walls were sometimes built with steps to upper floors. Inside, the people used ladders to climb between floors.

Materials

The early Pueblo people had no pack animals or
carts with wheels. They had to carry everything they
needed by hand—or on their backs. Their tools were
made from bones and stone, so it was hard for them to
work with some building materials. The Southwest is
rich in adobe clay and sandstone but poor in trees for
timber. It thus is not surprising that Pueblo dwellings
used lots of stone and adobe but little wood.

Being farmers, they did not move often. Therefore, it made sense for them to build houses that would last a long time. They wanted houses that would protect them and the food they stored from the summer heat. Stone and adobe were perfect materials for keeping out heat.

The early Pueblo people built mostly with sandstone bricks. Sandstone can be easily broken and shaped, even without metal tools. They shaped sandstone into bricks to build walls. They used adobe mud as mortar to hold stones together and fill gaps.

Stones are less common where the eastern Pueblos live, so those people used more adobe. They learned how to make adobe clay strong by mixing it with water and ashes. They shaped the mixture into bricks with their hands and dried the bricks in the sun.

When the Spanish ruled the Southwest, they showed the Pueblos how to make adobe bricks stronger by mixing in straw. They also showed the Pueblos how to make perfectly shaped bricks in wood frames. These improvements made adobe a better building material.

Using adobe to plaster the outsides of houses gave them all the same muddy brown color.

The Pueblo people had to walk great distances to find timber for ceiling beams and other purposes. Also, they did not have metal tools, so cutting and shaping wood was difficult. They therefore used wood only when they had to.

The outsides of houses were plastered over with adobe mud. They were rarely decorated. As a result, buildings were almost all the same muddy brown color. Interior walls, however, were usually painted white and were sometimes decorated with drawings and designs.

Building the House

In most Pueblo groups, married women owned the houses and did much of the work to build them. Men helped, too, especially in heavy work such as building roofs. The men also gathered most of the materials.

Whole pueblos were rarely planned in advance. They usually grew a little bit at a time. A new one-room house might be added to the pueblo after a couple was married and needed their own home. The new house might be built on the ground, or it might be built on top of the pueblo.

The builders began by marking on the ground where the walls were to go. Women then built up the walls by carefully stacking and fitting stones or adobe bricks together. After the walls were in place, the men helped place the beams for the roof. The women filled gaps between stones or bricks by pounding small stone pieces into openings. Then they plastered adobe over both the insides and outsides of the walls.

Living in Pueblos

Within pueblos, each house was usually the home of one family. Many houses were only one room, but some houses of larger families had two or three rooms. Married couples often lived with the brides' parents until they had their own houses.

Families that owned houses with more than one room generally reserved one room for sleeping and work and another room for storage. Food was always stored where it was away from the sun so it was protected from the heat.

Houses were simple. The rooms had a few pegs on the walls for hanging clothes and bedding. Perhaps there was a shelf or two. The people slept on blankets on the floors, not in beds. With small fires burning in corner fire pits, the houses were usually comfortable at night.

Food was often prepared inside, so baskets, pots, and kitchen utensils were stored inside. The inside walls were usually painted white to make the rooms brighter.

Villagers did most of their daily work and activities outdoors. They were thus almost always in contact with each other. Their feeling of belonging to a community was strengthened by festivals and ceremonies. In some pueblos buildings surrounded open areas in which festivals were held. Villagers would gather on rooftops to watch, as if they were sitting in a stadium.

During the days, most men went off to take care of the fields, where they grew corn (maize), beans, and cotton. Corn was very important to Pueblo communities. Corn is a nutritious grain, and it grew well in the dry Southwest. It could be easily dried, ground into meal for making bread, and stored through the winter season.

In the dry Southwest, reliable water supplies were important. The people became good at storing water. They stored it both in small containers, such as pots, and in reservoirs. In good years, their food and water stores lasted comfortably through the winters and dry months. In bad years, they might go hungry.

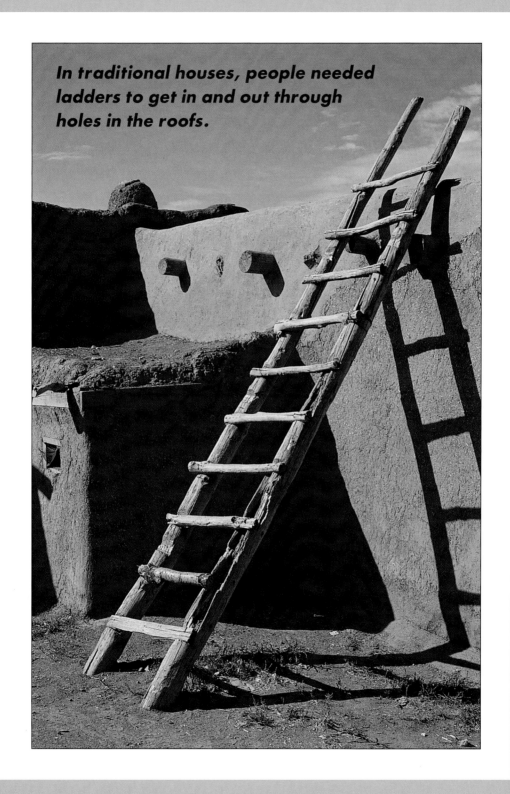

In traditional houses, people needed ladders to get in and out through holes in the roofs.

Kivas

Few ancient kivas still have their original roofs, which were made of wood beams, branches, and mud.

Every Pueblo village had several special community rooms called *kivas*. Kivas were round, instead of square, and were built mostly underground. Their floors were usually at least 5 feet (1.5 meters) below the surface of the ground. Flat stone slabs often lined the floors and sides. Sometimes stone benches were built along the sides.

Kivas could be as large as 25 feet (7.6 meters) across. Their roofs, like those of houses, were made of thick adobe supported by long wood beams and branches. Fire pits were cut in the centers of kivas. People climbed in and out of kivas on ladders placed in smoke holes cut through their roofs. Being partly underground, kivas were easier to keep warm than houses.

Each kiva belonged to a group of men who were related to one another. Kivas were used for religious ceremonies that only the men could attend. At other times, men used the kivas much like clubhouses, for relaxing or for doing light work.

Cliff Dwellings

Stone and adobe houses last a long time in the Southwest's dry climate. Ruins of thousands of houses built many centuries ago are still in good condition. The most spectacular of these are the *cliff dwellings* built in protected openings in sides of great mesas.

The Cliff Palace of Mesa Verde is one of the best-preserved cliff dwellings.

The ancient Anasazi people probably built these cliff dwellings for protection against enemies. It was hard for them to climb steep stone steps and ladders to reach their homes. However, their homes were easy to defend.

The Anasazi enjoyed comfortable lives when there was more rain in the Southwest. Toward the end of the thirteenth century, however, rainfall lessened. Cliff life became more difficult. Around 1300 the Anasazi suddenly moved away.

The Anasazi left most of their belongings behind. Overhanging cliffs protected their abandoned houses from rain and snow. Other people did not touch the houses until the late nineteenth century. The houses and their contents were well preserved. Today people can visit the ancient houses and see what life was like in the Southwest long ago.

Pueblos Today

Many Pueblo families still live in houses made of stone or adobe. A few live in very old buildings. One famous pueblo in Taos, New Mexico, has probably been lived in longer than any other building in North America.

Some Pueblo people still build houses in much the same way their ancestors did, with adobe bricks and timber beams. Now, however, they are likely to add plumbing, electricity, glass windows, and ground-level doors. Their roofs are also likely to be made of stronger materials, such as iron sheeting.

Modern pueblo buildings now are likely to have glass windows and ground-level doors.

Pueblo architecture has influenced modern building in the Southwest. On a visit to almost any Southwest city, one will see modern houses, stores, and even banks, made to look like traditional Pueblo houses. However, these buildings are made of wood, concrete, and steel—not real adobe.

Hundreds of Anasazi cliff dwellings and ancient pueblos can still be seen in national parks and other places, where they are being carefully protected.

Make a Model Pueblo

What you will need:

6 or more small cardboard boxes
tan or light brown poster paint
paintbrush
tape or glue
scissors

To make your pueblo:

1. Gather small cardboard boxes of similar sizes.

2. Cut tops and flaps off the boxes.

3. Set the boxes with their openings face down. Cut windows slits near the tops of their sides.

4. Cut ceiling holes in the roofs of ground-level boxes and cut low doorways in the sides of upper-story boxes.

5. Tape or glue the boxes together to form a pueblo. Set back the upper-story boxes so their doorways open onto the roofs of lower boxes.

6. Study the pictures in this book for other ideas to use.

7. Paint the boxes light brown.

Glossary

adobe: a word used to mean three related things: a heavy clay; bricks made from the clay; a building made from adobe bricks.

Anasazi: modern name for the ancient Southwest people who built the earliest pueblos and cliff dwellings. It is not known how they may be related to today's Pueblo peoples.

cliff dwellings: structures built in natural caves in the cliffs of sandstone mesas.

kiva: partly underground circular room used for special ceremonies.

mortar: moist, sticky compound used to hold building bricks or stones together and to fill gaps. Hardens when it dries.

pueblo: Spanish word for village. Used for both a village and a building complex within a village.

Pueblo: name given by the Spanish to Southwest Indians who lived in villages with stone and adobe buildings.

Further Reading

Burby, Liza N. *The Pueblo Indians.* New York: Chelsea Juniors, 1994.

Lavender, David. *Mother Earth, Father Sky: Pueblo Indians of the American Southwest.* New York: Holiday House, 1998.

Ortiz, Alfonso. *The Pueblo.* New York: Chelsea House, 1992.

Ross, Pamela. *The Pueblo Indians.* Mankato, Minn.: Bridgestone Books, 1999.

Shemie, Bonnie. *Houses of Adobe.* Plattsburgh, N.Y.: Tundra Books, 1995.

Yue, Charlotte, and David Yue. *The Pueblo.* Boston: Houghton Mifflin, 1986.

Suggested Web Sites

Mesa Verde National Park (National Park Service)
<www.nps.gov/meve>

On the Pueblo People
<www.desertusa.com/ind1/du_peo_pueblo.html>

On the Anasazi People
<www.desertusa.com/ind1/du_peo_ana.html>

Mythology of North American Indians
<msgc.engin.umich.edu/cgi-bin/tour>

American Indians and the Natural World
<www.clpgh.org/cmnh/exhibits/north-south-east-west/index.html>

Search Engine Source
<www/yahooligans.com/School_Bell/So...Studies/Cultures/Native_Americans/Tribes>

Index

Photo credits: Cover, pp. 8, 15, 21, Ben Klaffke; pp. 22, 24, PhotoDisc; p. 27, Marilyn "Angel" Wynn.